WILDLIFE IN BLOOM SERIES

Little Otter

BY AUTHOR & CONSERVATIONIST

LINDA BLACKMOOR

ISBN: 978-1-966417-23-1 (PRINT)

PUBLISHED BY QUILL PRESS. LINDA BLACKMOOR'S TITLES MAY BE PURCHASED IN BULK FOR EDUCATIONAL, BUSINESS, FUNDRAISING, OR SALES PROMOTIONAL USE. FOR INFORMATION, PLEASE EMAIL HELLO@LINDABLACKMOOR.COM

FIRST PRINT EDITION: 2025

LINDA BLACKMOOR
WWW.LINDABLACKMOOR.COM

SPECIES

Otters are playful, semi-aquatic mammals belonging to the Mustelidae family, which also includes weasels and badgers. There are 13 different otter species worldwide, such as the sea otter, giant otter, and river otter. They range in size from the small Asian small-clawed otter to the giant otter of South America. Each species has unique adaptations for life in water, like webbed feet and specialized fur.

FUR

Otters have dense, water-repellent fur made up of two layers—a soft underfur and an outer layer of guard hairs. This coat traps air to keep them warm and buoyant in chilly waters. Sea otters can have up to 1 million hairs per square inch, making theirs one of the thickest coats in the animal kingdom. Keeping their fur clean is vital for insulation, so otters groom often to maintain its protective qualities.

HABITAT

Different otter species thrive in freshwater rivers, lakes, wetlands, and coastal marine environments. They live on every continent except Australia and Antarctica, adapting to temperatures from icy subarctic waters to steamy tropical shores. Dens, called holts, are often built among rocks or roots near the water. Good habitat includes plenty of fish, healthy water, and safe places for raising young.

DIET

Otters are carnivores, feeding on fish, crustaceans, mollusks, and sometimes small mammals or birds. Sea otters are known for cracking open shellfish with rocks, while river otters often hunt crayfish in streams. A fast metabolism means they must eat frequently—sea otters can eat up to 25% of their body weight each day. By controlling prey, otters play an important role in maintaining healthy aquatic ecosystems.

TOOLS

Sea otters are one of the few mammals to use tools, often carrying small rocks in loose skin folds under their arms. They float on their backs, place shellfish on their bellies, and smash them open with the rock. This allows them to eat clams, mussels, and other hard-shelled creatures. Tool use showcases their intelligence and ability to solve feeding challenges in the wild.

SOCIAL

Otter behavior ranges from solitary in some river otter species to highly social among sea otters. Sea otters often float together in groups called "rafts," sometimes holding paws to avoid drifting apart. Giant otters live in family groups, hunting cooperatively in lakes and rivers. Social structures vary, but all otters rely on cooperation when raising young or maintaining safety in shared environments.

PUPS

Female otters give birth to one to five pups at a time, depending on the species. Sea otter pups are born in the water with thick, fluffy coats that keep them afloat until they learn to swim well. River otter pups stay in dens until they're strong enough to swim and follow their mothers. Baby otters learn essential survival skills from their parents, such as hunting and grooming.

FLOATING

Sea otters famously float on their backs, often using seaweed to anchor themselves and prevent drifting. They may sleep or rest this way, paddling gently to stay balanced. River otters can also float but generally stay more active, sliding in and out of rivers or streams. Floating helps conserve energy and keeps them safe from some predators lurking on shore.

ECOSYSTEM

Otters act as keystone species, meaning their presence helps balance entire ecosystems. Sea otters eat sea urchins, preventing the urchins from overgrazing kelp forests and protecting many marine creatures' habitats. River otters keep fish and crayfish populations healthy, which benefits water quality and other wildlife. Losing otters can cause harmful chain reactions in aquatic environments.

OTTER FACTS #10

WATER

Most otters are excellent swimmers, holding their breath for several minutes and diving to find prey. Their streamlined bodies and webbed feet help them chase fish through twisting currents. They can close their ears and nostrils underwater to prevent water intake. This aquatic skill set makes them formidable hunters in lakes, rivers, and coastlines.

OTTER FACTS #11

VOCALS

Otters communicate through chirps, whistles, growls, and scent markings to share information about territory and group members. Scent glands near their tails release strong odors, which they leave on rocks or logs. Sea otters also use body language, such as rubbing faces or pawing at each other, to signal requests or warnings. Communication ensures they can coordinate hunts and maintain social ties.

OTTER FACTS #12

ADAPT

Otters show great adaptability, living in both saltwater and freshwater habitats across different climates. They adjust their hunting strategies based on local prey, using speed, agility, or tool use as needed. Their fur and body shape protect them from cold waters and strong currents. This versatility allows otters to thrive in environments ranging from coastal kelp forests to forest streams.

OTTER FACTS #13

LIFESPAN

In the wild, otters typically live 8 to 12 years, though sea otters can sometimes reach their mid-teens. Threats include predators like sharks, bald eagles (for pups), pollution, and habitat loss. Otters in human care can live longer, often surpassing 15 years with proper diet and veterinary care. Their lifespan reflects both natural challenges and the importance of conservation efforts.

www.ingramcontent.com/pod-product-compliance
Lightning Source LLC
Chambersburg PA
CBHW060837270326
41933CB00002B/119